A Wild Onion Dinner

by Celeste Keys

Illustrated by Fabricio Vanden Broeck

Glenview, Illinois • Boston, Massachusetts • Chandler, Arizona
Upper Saddle River, New Jersey

David and Marco met after school.
"Let's play baseball," said Marco.
"I have to dig wild onions," said
David. "Come with me!"

creek

wild
onion plants

stick

The boys went to the creek. Their moms went too.

They looked for wild onions. David's mom used a stick to dig.

onion

"Why do you dig onions?"
asked Marco.
"We will have a Wild Onion Dinner,"
said David. "You can come."

"It is our tradition. We do this every year," said David. "We are Muscogee Native Americans."

"We eat onions in spring," said David. "We eat them to get ready for summer."

"I want to eat wild onions too," said Marco.

Wild Onion Dinner

Marco and his mom went to the dinner. They were ready for the Wild Onion Dinner.

"The food is great," said Marco.
"It is!" said David. "Now we will be ready for summer and baseball."